MARIAN ANDERSON

MARIAN ANDERSON

by Tobi Tobias

illustrated by Symeon Shimin

THOMAS Y. CROWELL COMPANY

NEW YORK

CROWELL BIOGRAPHIES
Edited by Susan Bartlett Weber

JANE ADDAMS *by Gail Faithfull Keller*
MARIAN ANDERSON *by Tobi Tobias*
LEONARD BERNSTEIN *by Molly Cone*
MARTHA BERRY *by Mary Kay Phelan*
WILT CHAMBERLAIN *by Kenneth Rudeen*
CESAR CHAVEZ *by Ruth Franchere*
SAMUEL CLEMENS *by Charles Michael Daugherty*
CHARLES DREW *by Roland Bertol*
FANNIE LOU HAMER *by June Jordan*
FIORELLO LA GUARDIA *by Mervyn Kaufman*
THE MAYO BROTHERS *by Jane Goodsell*
JOHN MUIR *by Charles P. Graves*
GORDON PARKS *by Midge Turk*
THE RINGLING BROTHERS *by Molly Cone*
JACKIE ROBINSON *by Kenneth Rudeen*
ELEANOR ROOSEVELT *by Jane Goodsell*
MARIA TALLCHIEF *by Tobi Tobias*
JIM THORPE *by Thomas Fall*
THE WRIGHT BROTHERS *by Ruth Franchere*
MALCOLM X *by Arnold Adolf*

Copyright © 1972 by Tobi Tobias
Illustrations copyright © 1972 by Symeon Shimin

All rights reserved. Except for use in a review, the reproduction or utilization of this work in any form or by any electronic, mechanical, or other means, now known or hereafter invented, including xerography, photocopying, and recording, and in any information storage and retrieval system is forbidden without the written permission of the publisher. Published simultaneously in Canada by Fitzhenry & Whiteside Limited, Toronto.

Manufactured in the United States of America
L.C. Card 79-139101   ISBN 0-690-51846-3   0-690-51847-1 (LB)
2 3 4 5 6 7 8 9 10

MARIAN ANDERSON

In a small house in Philadelphia a three-year-old girl was singing. She sat at a little table that she liked to make believe was her piano. The walls of the room were covered with flowered paper. The child thought she saw friendly faces in the flowers, looking down at her as she played and sang. The child's name was Marian Anderson. When she grew up, she became one of the world's best-loved singers.

Marian was born on February 27, 1903. Her father, John Anderson, worked long hours delivering coal and ice. Her mother, Anna Anderson, had been a schoolteacher once. Now she was busy keeping the house comfortable for her husband and their three daughters: Marian, Alyce, and Ethel. The Anderson family did not have much money, but they cared about each other and had many happy times together.

As Marian grew older, her father took her to church with him every Sunday. The Union Baptist Church was important to the people in Marian's neighborhood. Often their lives were unhappy. Many of them were poor. Some of them had trouble getting jobs. In church they heard words and music that said to them: "Yes, you have troubles. We know that life can be hard. We must hope for good things to come."

Marian joined the children's choir of the church. As she sang with this group, the choirmaster noticed her beautiful voice. He asked her to practice a duet with her best friend, Viola Johnson. The next Sunday the two girls stood up to sing for the whole congregation. It was Marian's first public performance. She was six years old.

Marian was finding out about music in other ways, too. When she was eight, her father bought an old piano. But there was no money for music

lessons. After weeks of trying, Marian taught herself to play simple tunes. She wished she could learn more.

Then one day she saw a used violin in a store window. She went in and asked the man how much it cost. "Three dollars and ninety-five cents," he said. "Is it a good violin?" Marian asked. She knew how hard it would be for her to get that much money. "Oh, it's a very fine instrument," the storekeeper said.

Marian went to work after school. She scrubbed steps for her neighbors and ran their errands. If someone gave her a few cents for candy, she put the money carefully away. At last she earned and saved enough nickels and pennies. Proudly she went back to the store and bought the violin. A friend of the family taught her to tune it and to play a few notes. But before long the strings snapped and the wood of the violin cracked. It was no good at all. Marian

was sad and disappointed. She wanted so much to make music well.

Still she was never downhearted for long. She loved singing in the choir. Her full, rich voice poured through the church. The sound she made was so loud the choirmaster sometimes laughed and said, "Hold back a little there, Marian. We

want to hear the other singers, too." Friends and neighbors in the congregation, though, had nothing but praise for Marian.

Her voice was deep and velvety, the kind musicians call contralto. But she could reach up to the high soprano notes, too, and even down to the low music of the baritone. When the choir prepared a new song, Marian learned all the different parts, high and low, not just her own. Then, if a singer could not come to church on Sunday, she helped out by singing in his place. It made her happy to know the choir needed her, and she learned a lot about music this way.

Secretly she dreamed of being a singer when she grew up.

At home, life was good. The Andersons were a warm, close family. Even though Marian's father worked hard and came home tired, he was always ready to laugh and joke with his daughters. Sometimes he surprised them with special treats, like new Easter hats or tickets to the circus. And Mrs. Anderson was there whenever the girls needed her, teaching them and loving them.

But when Marian was twelve, her father died. Life changed then. Harder times began. Marian's mother had to go out to work. She got a job cleaning other people's houses and bringing their laundry home to wash and iron. Mrs. Anderson was a frail, gentle woman, but she had great spirit. No matter how difficult her tasks were, she never complained. Somehow she found the extra strength to make a good home for her children.

As the years went by, Marian began to realize

how hard her mother worked to provide for her family. "I'm getting old enough now," she thought, "I must do something, too." When she entered high school she tried to study useful subjects, like typing. She knew this would help her get a job as a secretary in an office. But all the time her heart was really set on singing.

If only she could earn enough money at it, she could make singing her life's work. Of course she was not paid for singing in church. Ever since she was eight, though, she had been invited to sing in other churches, too. People all over Philadelphia got to know about her splendid voice. They began asking her to perform at their parties and club meetings. By the time Marian was in high school, she was getting $5.00 every time she sang at one of these gatherings.

This seemed like a lot of money to her. Yet she knew she was still a long way from being a professional singer. She had been born with a fine voice and she sang with deep feeling. But Marian saw how much she still had to learn. The best way, she decided, would be to have lessons, at a music school.

Early one morning she took the trolley car to a well-known school in uptown Philadelphia. She went into the building and got in line with a group of girls who were waiting to apply. When Marian's turn came, the pretty, blue-eyed woman in charge paid no attention to her. Marian stepped aside. After everyone else had been taken care of, the woman said, "What do *you* want?" in a sharp voice. "I'd like to arrange for lessons, please—" Marian began politely. "We don't take colored," said the woman coldly, and turned away.

Marian felt hurt and confused. She had often heard that white people sometimes behaved in this cruel, thoughtless way toward Negroes. But it had never really happened to her before. In her neighborhood black people and white people lived side by side. Most of the time they were comfortable and friendly with each other. True enough, their skins were different, Marian thought, but not their feelings.

Sadly she went home to tell her mother what happened at the school. "The way that woman spoke," she cried, "it bit into my soul." Her mother listened quietly. Was she wrong to think a Negro girl could become a singer? Marian asked. Maybe her dreams were foolish.

Mrs. Anderson thought for a while. Then, in her calm, sure way, she said, "Of course you can be a singer, Marian. You must have faith. There will be another way for you to learn what you need to know."

And there was another way. The people at the Union Baptist Church believed in Marian's talent. These friends and neighbors planned a concert to help her. Every bit of money they got

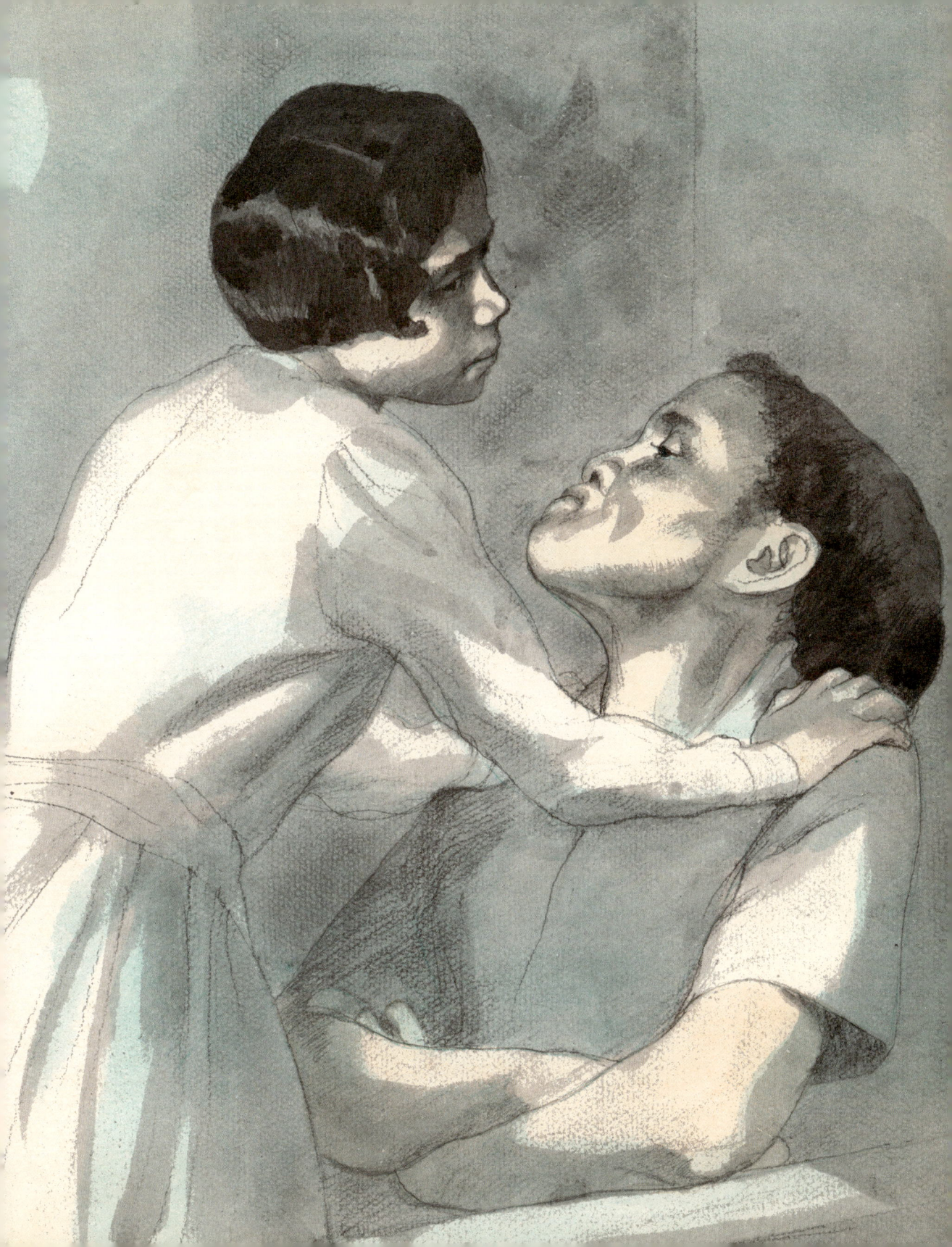

from the tickets was set aside to pay for private singing lessons for Marian.

Marian performed at the concert herself, but the main star was Roland Hayes. Mr. Hayes was the first Negro singer to become famous in the concert halls of America and Europe. He sang the spirituals Marian and her people knew so well. These were powerful songs of sorrow, of joy, and of hope that the Negroes made up when they were slaves. Mr. Hayes also sang lieder, poems set to music by the great European composers. Marian could not understand the French or German languages they were sung in. Still she was quick to hear the beauty of the music. She longed to learn such songs herself.

Then, as she listened to Mr. Hayes's pure tenor voice, she suddenly realized, "His skin is dark, like mine. And he has gone so far. They say he has even sung for kings and queens. If he can, perhaps I can too." Slowly, from this time on,

Marian's pride began to grow. It was never an angry pride, but full of faith and hope. Throughout her life, no matter what happened, it kept her strong.

With the money raised at the concert, Marian started taking music lessons. She quickly learned everything her teachers could show her. Then Giuseppi Boghetti agreed to listen to her. He was a well-known voice coach with studios in Philadelphia and New York. At first he spoke

to her gruffly. "I am seeing you just as a favor," he said. "I don't want any new students. I have too many already."

Marian sang for him. The deep beauty and feeling in her voice instantly changed Mr. Boghetti's mind. "I will make room for you right away," he declared. "Don't think it will be easy, though. You have a grand voice. But it must be trained, so that it can do whatever you want it to do. For this you need many exercises and much

hard practicing. We will work together. After that you will be able to go anywhere and sing for anybody."

That year Marian finished high school. With more free time, she could do more performing. She began to travel farther from home to sing in churches, colleges, and small theaters. Finally she earned enough money to make one of her greatest wishes come true. The day came when she could say to her mother, "I can take care of you now. You don't have to work any more." Afterward Marian always said that was the happiest day of her life.

When Mr. Boghetti thought Marian was ready, he let her enter a contest of three hundred young singers. The first prize was a chance to perform with the New York Philharmonic Orchestra. By now Marian's amazing voice was well trained. And, as always, she put her whole spirit into the music. After she sang, the other contestants clapped and cheered. Then the judges announced that she had won.

Marian hoped this prize would prove she was ready to sing in America's best concert halls. The people who wrote about music in the newspapers and magazines were beginning to say fine things about her. But several years passed and still she was not often asked to sing in the really important theaters. Most Americans just did not want to believe that a Negro could be an excellent concert singer. They would not give Marian a chance to show them how good she was.

Marian felt that her career was standing still. "What can I do about this?" she wondered. Finally she decided to go to Europe. There she would study with famous singing masters. Then, if she performed for European audiences, and these people liked her work, perhaps America would welcome her back and realize what she could do.

She studied first in England. Then she went to

Germany, to learn the language of her favorite lieder. There she met Kosti Vehanen, a pianist from Finland. "Let me become your accompanist," he offered. Marian agreed. Kosti would play the piano while she sang. Together they set out on a tour of the Scandinavian countries in the north of Europe. Here—in Norway, Sweden, Finland, and Denmark—Marian was immediately accepted as a great singer by everyone who heard her. It did not matter to these people that Marian was black and most of them were white. They loved her voice and they loved her.

A tour of Europe followed. Once again Marian was a huge success. Arturo Toscanini, the famous orchestra conductor, came to one of her concerts. He was so moved by her singing that he went backstage afterward to speak to her. Marian could hardly believe what he said: "A voice like yours is heard only once in a hundred years."

Ordinary people had the same feeling about

her. It was Marian's way to end each of her concerts with a group of Negro spirituals. Often the Europeans could not understand the English words. It made no difference. Marian poured the heart and soul of her people into this music. When the songs she planned to sing were over, the audience would not leave the theater. They called for her again and again. Some of them rushed down the aisles and pounded on the stage, shouting out the names of the spirituals they liked best. "'Deep River'!" they yelled. "'Heaven, Heaven'!"

Never in America had she had a welcome like this. And yet Marian thought it was time to go back to her own country. Her stay in Europe helped her find her place as a singer. But America was her home. Her family was there. All the people who first believed in her and helped her were there, waiting. She knew she must return to them.

Marian sailed back to the United States on a large ocean liner. Every day she and Kosti practiced together for the important homecoming concert in New York. One morning, as Marian was going down the staircase to the rehearsal room, the rough sea made the ship lurch. Marian lost her balance and fell. She was in great pain. The doctor told her she had a broken bone in her foot. He put her leg in a bulky plaster cast.

But Marian did not disappoint the people who came to her concert. On December 30, 1935, she sang at Town Hall. Her cast was hidden by a long evening dress. And this time her American audience let themselves understand what a wonderful singer this black woman was. Marian sang about the beautiful things in the world, and the ugly things. She sang about happy times and sad ones. She sang about the deepest thoughts and feelings that all people share. When she finished there was a long silence. Then the audience rose to its feet and burst into wild applause.

In the next thirty years Marian sang all over the world. She traveled across the United States again and again. She went back to Europe many times. She gave concerts in Russia, Israel, and Japan. She was almost always accepted as she deserved. Sometimes, though, there were difficulties because she was black. But when others were mean-spirited, Marian knew how to be generous and understanding. Once, when she faced this kind of trouble, the whole world was watching.

In the spring of 1939 she planned to give a concert in Washington, D.C., the nation's capital. She hoped to appear in Constitution Hall. It was owned by the Daughters of the American Revolution, a group of women whose families had, long ago, fought for freedom in the United States. But the D.A.R. refused to let Marian Anderson sing on their stage. Why? There could be only one answer. She was a Negro.

Fair-minded people all over America said this was wrong. Throughout the world men and women waited to see what would happen. Marian was not a fighter. But through her music she would do whatever she could to gain freedom and justice for her people. Leaders of the United States government invited her to give her concert outdoors for everyone who wanted to come. On Easter Sunday Marian came to the Lincoln Memorial. She stood before the statue of Abraham Lincoln, the president who freed the Negro slaves. There she sang for 75,000 people. Black and white together, they joined her in the opening song—"The Star-Spangled Banner."

Four years later Marian married Orpheus Fisher. They had known each other for a long time. Together they chose some beautiful land in the Connecticut farm country. On it they built the simple, comfortable house Marian had always dreamed of. Close by, near a running brook, was a separate studio for Marian to work in. Mr. Fisher, who was an architect, designed everything himself.

Now, although Marian might be on tour most of the year, she always came home to Marianna Farm for the summer. There, with her new accompanist, Franz Rupp, she prepared her concerts for the next season. First Marian and Franz carefully picked out the songs they wanted to do. Then they studied them and practiced them over and over again. They tried to make their performance of each song as close to perfect as they could.

Marianna Farm was also a place of rest. Here Marian could relax with her husband. She enjoyed sewing things for her home and caring for the pet animals they kept. Here, too, her mother and sisters often visited with her.

After twenty years as a successful concert singer, Marian was given a chance to try another kind of music. In 1955 she was asked to appear with the world-famous Metropolitan Opera Company in New York. She took the part of Ulrica, the gypsy fortune-teller, in Verdi's opera *The Masked Ball*. It was the first time a Negro had sung an important role at the Metropolitan as a regular company member.

Marian's part was not easy. She had to reach very high and very low notes, and join in difficult group singing. And as she sang, she had to make the audience believe she was truly a gypsy sorceress. The whole company worked with her. Marian said it was like being part of a big fam-

ily. Together they gave a wonderful performance of the opera.

That night, as the gold curtain came down at the Met, people called excitedly, "Anderson, Anderson!" Some of them even cried, thinking of all Marian had done to reach this great moment. That night a new audience discovered her glorious voice. More important, Marian opened a door for her own people. From that time on, Negro singers were welcome on the great opera stage.

Marian's talent and her simple, beautiful spirit brought her many honors. Like Roland Hayes, she sang for kings and queens, and for three presidents of the United States. Two of her best rewards, though, were jobs she was invited to do.

In 1951 the American government asked her to tour the countries of Asia. She sang to the people and then spoke with them. These men and women found it easy to talk to her, to tell her the thoughts deep inside them, to explain what

their countries needed and what they hoped for. Marian understood people from different places so well that she was then sent to the United Nations. There she joined the leaders of many countries in trying to bring peace to the world.

Now Marian was growing older. Her singing voice was not as rich and full as it used to be. Of course she would always sing at home, for her family and friends. But it was best to end the days of performing.

In 1956 she made a farewell tour of Europe and America. As she took her last bows from the stage, she thought, "My work is not over. There is still much I can do. I want to help people of different groups come to understand each other. I can make the way easier for young singers. I want to do something for children all over the world—with my hands, and my heart, and my soul. In a way, my work is just beginning."

ABOUT THE AUTHOR

Tobi Tobias lives in a renovated brownstone on New York's Upper West Side with her husband Irwin, her son John, her daughter Anne, and a varying number of small domestic animals. She likes children, writing, New York, ballet, mystery stories, paintings, questions, and spaghetti.

ABOUT THE ILLUSTRATOR

Symeon Shimin was born in Astrakhan, on the Caspian Sea, in Russia, and came to the United States with his family ten years later. Although he attended art classes at Cooper Union and also painted in the studio of George Luks, Mr. Shimin is primarily self-taught; he says that he found his best schooling in the museums and art galleries in this country and in France and Spain.

Mr. Shimin was especially motivated in his illustrations for this book. Upon hearing Marian Anderson in concert, he found her singing "an extraordinarily rich experience. Something wonderful came through for which I felt privileged and thankful."